Midge's mum wanted some eggs.

Midge went to the egg shop.

He put the eggs in a bag.

"Come and play,"
said his friends.

"I can't," said Midge. "My Mum
wants these eggs."

Midge saw his friend. The friend had a go-kart.

Midge wanted a go.

Midge put the bag down.

He went on the go-kart. He
forgot the eggs.

A man put the bag in the cart.
"Oh no!" said Midge. "The eggs!"

Midge's mum looked at the bag.

"Sorry, Mum," said Midge.

Midge's mum went to the egg shop. She got some more eggs.

14

She put the eggs in a basket.

Oh no!